AUDIOVISUAL TRAINING
MODULES

The Instructional Design Library

Volume 4

AUDIOVISUAL TRAINING MODULES

Harold D. Stolovitch
Universite de Montreal

Danny G. Langdon
Series Editor

Educational Technology Publications
Englewood Cliffs, New Jersey 07632

Library of Congress Cataloging in Publication Data

Stolovitch, Harold D
   Audiovisual training modules.

   (The Instructional design library; v. no. 4)
   Bibliography: p.
   1. Audio-visual education. 2. Programmed
instruction. I. Title. II. Series.
LB1043.S87   371.33   77-25142
ISBN 0-87778-108-7

Printed in the United States of America.

Library of Congress Catalog Card Number: 77-25142.

International Standard Book Number: 0-87778-108-7.

First Printing: February, 1978.

FOREWORD

It has always been, to my way of thinking, a little strange that so little has been done in the visual area of instruction to make this medium truly interactive. I refer to structured interaction toward learning and testing oneself, rather than an informal interaction of becoming involved in the presentation. Writing and audio, as other media forms, have made far more use of improving effectiveness by provisions for student-content-medium interaction. Of course, I recognize, at the same time that visual media involving motion are limited, because of the motion, in provisions for allowing interaction. I am pleased to see that Harold D. Stolovitch has made some progress in this regard and that he clearly explains and illustrates this for us.

I believe that the reader will find this book highly functional. It tells and illustrates what the instructional design can be, and an added amount of explanation has been given regarding how to go about developing Audiovisual Training Modules. At the first-draft manuscript stage, the author suggested that the Developmental Guide section be shortened, but my own feeling that his first draft had much to offer persuaded him otherwise. I think you will agree. Those in need of bringing audiovisual combinations to their students' needs will find this book very much worth the time needed to fully absorb its contents.

Danny G. Langdon
Series Editor

PREFACE

Where do audiovisual modules come from? Hardly a question a child might ask, but one any instructional developer might be required to answer. Essentially, two main paths have led to the emergence of the audiovisual training module design: a constantly growing awareness of the important contribution audiovisual materials can make to education and training, and the accompanying realization that systematically developed materials can help students to learn effectively. The movement away from large-group, teacher-centered curricula to more individualized instructional settings and the rise of competency-based programs have also fostered a need for alternative instructional designs. It is my firm conviction that the audiovidual training module, as a cost-effective, motivating, and relatively easy-to-use form of instruction, is destined to increase in popularity. Studies have demonstrated its effectiveness in helping learners attain prespecified and often complex objectives. Experience shows that students enjoy learning by means of such modules.

During the past several years, I have participated in the development of a large number of audiovisual training modules. The examples in this book are for the most part illustrative of the products teachers and trainers with whom I have worked have turned out. What has impressed me again and again is the power of the design, not only in terms of its effects on the student, but also in the way it can help change the instructor who develops a module. This last point is, perhaps, the most exciting of all. Having produced an audio-visual training module, with its demands of sticking to the essentials and viewing instruction entirely from the learner's point of view, a teacher or trainer can never again be the same. There is a change—and it is always for the better!

I should never have been able to write this volume if it had not been for three factors and three people:

(1) the freedom given to me to test my ideas at the Center for Innovation in Teaching the Handicapped under the direction of Melvyn I. Semmel, an educator of great vision;

(2) the confidence of my immediate superior, guru, and beloved colleague, Sivasailam Thiagarajan, genius; and

(3) the technical training, advice, expertise, and constant encouragement of Dennis Pett, director of instructional services, Indiana University, and one of the world's finest instructional materials designers. To these three gentlemen, truly dedicated to effective learning, I dedicate this work.

H.D.S.

CONTENTS

ABSTRACT

AUDIOVISUAL TRAINING MODULES

Audiovisual training modules are known by a variety of names—sound-slide-response book sets, multi-media packages, AV learning packages, and so on. Essentially, the audiovisual training module design consists of three elements: an audiotape or cassette, a set of visuals (either slides or a filmstrip), and a response book which permits the trainee to actively participate in the instruction.

Whereas the sound-slide presentation is "old hat," the audiovisual training module offers some singular aspects which allow the design to reply to many of the needs of competency based programs. The audiovisual training module depends on systematic development procedures. It offers an effective and proven format for individualized programs, although it is flexible enough to be utilized in a variety of configurations. It responds to the necessity of multisensory education. It permits self-pacing. And it offers an affective dimension often absent in other designs.

This book provides an introduction to the audiovisual training module design. It explains how the audiovisual training module can be used. It describes what subjects it can handle, and presents copious examples across a variety of fields and levels. It contains guidelines for producing your own modules.

AUDIOVISUAL TRAINING
MODULES

I.

USE

So much instruction comes to us via print materials and lectures, that we often welcome any deviation from this time-honored practice as blessed relief. Despite a constant stream of innovative alternative designs to teacher and textbook, by and large the traditional classroom of past centuries remains the dominant instructional vehicle of today. This brief volume sets out with the express purpose of providing the teacher with another viable and effective approach to instruction—the audiovisual training module. Its antecedents are the "slide show," which teachers have used for years to illustrate their lectures; the filmstrip, which has been a common classroom aid for providing visual information about a given topic; and the audiotape, which offers students spoken commentaries. The role we usually assign to all of these media is that of teaching *aids*—ancillary materials to support the teacher and to make his/her instruction more effective. Only recently have innovative instructors been combining these assorted media into a unified package whose function is to *carry the main instructional load.*

Why is this combination type of instructional design receiving increased attention? There are several excellent reasons. The audiovisual training module is an extremely flexible instructional vehicle. It meets two distinct needs of today's classroom—individualization and self-pacing. In addition, many instructors have found that pairs of students, small groups, or even entire assembly halls can also effectively learn from audiovisual training modules. This flexibility to meet a variety of delivery and content requirements makes the AV training module one of the most useful instructional design processes.

The audiovisual training module has three intertwined components. Slides or filmstrips, audiocassette or tape, and response book combine to cover a wide range of media attributes. Figure 1 shows the attributes contained in the usual instructional media found in schools and training centers. The check marks have been placed beside those attributes which the audiovisual training module combination possesses. As you can see from the figure, taken together, the slides/filmstrip, audiocassette/tape, and print response book cover all attributes except for motion and three-dimensionality. This suggests that for virtually all types of training and instruction, other than those requiring motion or actual manipulation and handling, the AV module stands as a logical and attractive instructional design.

Several other features of this design which make its use very pertinent to most instructional settings also require elaboration. The AV module is a multi-channel device providing instruction both visually and auditorally. Students can make responses, interact with the instruction, and receive feedback. They can get close-up views and sounds. With advances in inexpensive yet reliable hardware (the interm for audiovisual equipment) the audiovisual module has become extremely portable. A number of viewers for AV modules are light and compact, facilitating use in the home or almost any setting. The AV module also makes for a novel alternative to daily classroom instruction. As will be demonstrated later, learners can also be brought into the design process so that learning can take place through doing (i.e.,

Figure 1

Media Most Frequently Found in Schools and Training Centers and Their Attributes

Media most commonly found in schools and training centers ←

Media attributes ↓

Media attributes	Audiotape	Print	Realia	Slides/filmstrip	Overhead transparency	Super-8 filmloop	16mm film	Videotape	CAI terminal
√ Audio	X					X	/	X	/
√ Visual		X	X	X	X	X	X	X	X
Motion				/		X	X	X	/
√ Color		X	X	X	X	X	X	/	/
3-Dimensionality			X						
√ Response acceptance	X	X							X
√ Feedback capacity	X	X		X	/	/	/	/	X
√ Self-pacing	/	X	X	X					X
√ Random access		X	X	X	/				X
√ Self-contained	X	X	X	X		X	X	X	X
√ Easy-to-use	X	X	X	X	X		X	/	X
√ Inexpensive	X	X		X	X				
√ Quick to set up	X	X	/	X	X		X	/	
√ No special environment	X	X	X	/			X	X	
√ Grouping flexible	X	X	X	X			/	X	/
√ Easy handling/storage	X	X		X	X	X	X	X	
√ Generally available	X	X		X	X	/			

X = is usually associated with the medium
/ = can be obtained

participation in the preparation of an AV module). Finally, one important factor which should be stressed is that compared with many other forms of instructional media production, audiovisual training modules can be produced on a relatively inexpensive basis with locally available talent and with minimal costs.

What subjects lend themselves best to the audiovisual training module design? As pointed out earlier, the wide range of media attributes, the flexible delivery possibilities, and the portability of the package make its use appropriate for a wide range of content. Virtually anything that requires visualization is a suitable topic. Subjects that require the student to both see and hear are especially appropriate. Instruments of the orchestra, interview techniques, animal identification, and foreign languages are obvious candidates for this design. Historical themes, geographic voyages, or scientific procedures can also make ideal use of the audiovisual training module design. Where an instructor is concerned with building emotional as well as cognitive response on the part of his students, music, sound effects, and close-ups of facial expressions can emphasize and enhance particular points. For example, one segment of an audiovisual training module on designing classroom visual materials for practicing teachers takes the trainee on a tour of a school. Visual materials in a number of classrooms are shown from a variety of angles. Smiling children are also included in many of the shots. Accompanying this 20-second tour is light-hearted music. Teachers seeing this segment generally loosen up and appear more prepared to start on the task of designing their own visuals.

It is necessary to emphasize that the audiovisual training module is not an instructional panacea. Competencies requiring physical dexterity, taking apart and putting together, or analysis of a movement (e.g., a ballet leap) are not especially suitable for the type of design described in this book, although parts of these topics may be appropriate where still pictures can capture a critical aspect of a movement while verbal commentary clarifies.

One major advantage of the audiovisual training module is that of self-pacing. This book on audiovisual training modules offers a useful alternative to the type of classroom teaching where the teacher is always in command. The audiovisual training module is in the hands of the students who control the buttons which turn the instruction on and off. This means that a student can stop the tape to study a visual, rewind and review a section he or she did not quite understand, or even shut the instruction off for a while and clear his or her head before continuing. To illustrate this point, students working through an AV module on selecting correct filters for their photography (a rather complex topic involving multiple discriminations at many decision points) may return to earlier fundamental principles, reexamine visuals showing specific filters and their effects, or even shut down the module, shoot and develop some photographs, and return to the module for comparisons.

If any one major change has occurred which has fostered the increased use of audiovisual training modules, it has been in the area of hardware. Individual or small-group viewers with both visual and synchronized audio capabilities are now available from a number of reputable firms at prices as low as $100 when purchased in quantity. What is most impressive about these viewing units is their extreme portability and durability. One popular model is no larger than an encyclopedia volume and weighs only six pounds, yet can handle a filmstrip and a synchronized audio-cassette, advance automatically, accept earphones, and operate under normal lighting conditions. Its price is just over $100.

One reason why use of the audiovisual training module has grown is because of the ease with which even young children can use it. Whether with filmstrip or slides, it takes only a few seconds to start up. Many newer machines can be pulsed to stop automatically when a student is asked to make a response. Since many libraries, resource centers, training laboratories, and schools are equipping themselves with these devices, the accessibility and familiarity of the machines to learners has made the audiovisual training module an instructional design within reach of almost every instructor. The fact that these modules can be used almost anywhere there is an electrical outlet (and there are even battery models, too) increases the use in a variety of instructional situations, such as where there is limited space or nonspecialized facilities, where there are homebound or bedridden learners, where learners wish to take instruction home or to the job, or where individually scheduled, competency-based programs have been instituted.

To summarize, then, audiovisual training modules have application in a wide variety of contexts. Because they are concerned with specific skills and competencies, they are a natural design to select for any competency-based program. The audiovisual training module encompasses a broad range of media attributes, making it a viable instructional vehicle for any topic which does not specifically require the display of motion or three-dimensionality. It lends itself to instruction which requires affective responses in addition to pure cognitive learning. The design is most suited to individualized, self-paced instruction, but it is flexible enough for larger group use. It requires some hardware support, but much less costly production and viewing equipment than either film or video. It can be employed where facilities are limited and portability is a must. And it can be set up and used by any type of learner from preschooler to adult.

Finally, and most importantly, an audiovisual training module design consisting of slides or filmstrip, audiocassette or tape, and response books can be developed and produced locally with a minimum of specialized skills.

II.

OPERATIONAL DESCRIPTION

What is an audiovisual training module? Physically it is a small, self-contained package composed of a set of visuals, an audiotape of some sort, and a printed response book. The whole set can be stored in a container no larger than an average sized book. What makes this a unique and effective instructional design is: the number of media attributes contained by the powerful combination, the flexibility of use, and the systematic method of uniting the components into an instructional tool which results in competency attainment. Each component has a unique function within the module. The combination of the three provides a synergistic output that goes beyond the sum of the effects of the individual parts. This chapter examines the components of the audiovisual training module and describes how they all fit together.

The primary rationale for combining slides or filmstrip with audiotape and response booklet is twofold: (1) The combination meets a wide range of instructional needs. (2) It delivers almost as much instructional impact as other media which are more costly, more difficult to produce, and which require more equipment and skills for delivery.

The response book is the prime component of the design. It usually takes the form of a duplicated workbook style booklet. In it are contained the objectives of the module, criterion items perfectly matching each objective, with ample space for trainee responses, rules, principles, and tips which the trainee may need to refer to at a later time, and useful references for those who want additional materials. This response book is the consumable part of the module. After completing the mediated parts and the exercises, the trainee takes it away with him as a permanent and personal record. The response book is the trainee's link with the audio and visual portions of the module. The narration and visuals make frequent reference to the response book. The trainee replies on its pages then returns for feedback, extended explanations, and additional examples of correct responses. Key concepts, charts, procedures, and checklists are reproduced in the response book.

While the response book acts as the integrating and guiding component of the audiovisual training module, and as the source for both objectives and criterion items, the audio portion takes on the major instructional load. Once the trainee turns on the machine, it is the audiotape which directs his/her attention, provides most of the directions, explanations and examples, and guides the trainee's activities. In the DESIGN FORMAT chapter of this book, deriving the structure and sequence for an audiovisual training module will be discussed in detail. At this point it must be stressed that essential to the effectiveness of this type of module design is a careful analysis of the major competency to be acquired by the trainee who uses the package. This analysis acts as the base for setting out the specific objectives contained in the response book. Once these objectives are converted to criterion items, the audio script is written with the exclusive intent of leading the trainee directly, efficiently, and in as motivating a manner as possible to the criterion items in the response book. Taking as an example a fifth grade audiovisual training module on using a pocket calculator to convert fractions into decimals, the specific performance objective in the response book states:

Given a six function (+, −, x, +, x^2, %) pocket calculator the student will be able to correctly convert a simple fraction to a decimal.

The script then carries the instructional steps in simple, straightforward language as it encourages the student to "press along" with the audiotape. After providing sufficient guidance to the student, the tape directs him/her to the response book criterion item, where he/she finds a series of conversions to try:

Using your own calculator, convert these simple fractions to decimals: 1/8, 3/5, 7/17, 9/123. When you have done this, turn the tape back on.

The student completes the exercise and then returns to the audiotape where feedback and commentary is provided.

The role of the visuals is threefold. The main purpose is to help the trainee see what is meant by a particular explanation or step. Take, for example, the module previously described on using the pocket calculator. While the audio component states: "Place your right first finger on the key marked "x" located at the right ..." a slide appears showing the key board with a child's finger pointing toward that key. After the operation when the narrator states "The lighted number display should look like this ..." a close up slide of the display part of the pocket calculator, showing the correct sequence of digits, appears before the youngster.

Another major function of the visual component is that of providing a "reality base" and models with whom trainees can identify. In a module on job interviews, real employers, personnel managers, and working people are seen. Young job hunters resembling a cross-section of the target audience (senior high school students) are shown preparing, grooming, adjusting, smiling, etc. As the audiotape describes a situation or presents a dialogue, the visuals focus in on relevant cues. As an example, the audiotape tells the student: "Look composed during the interview. Don't move your hands around or play with objects. Keep them still in your lap if you don't know what to do with them." A slide of a composed young woman, hands neatly folded in lap, is displayed. This element of realism offers a dimension that a classroom lecture or a printed page cannot easily convey.

The third important role of the visual is to focus attention on specific key parts or examples or provide opportunities for visual discriminations. Drawing from a module on criterion-referenced testing, one segment deals with matching criterion items to objectives. The trainees are directed to examine an objective and two alternative items a designer has come up with. The visual contains the following words:

OBJECTIVE: Using a standard four-function pocket calculator, DIVIDE by any given two-digit number.

CRITERION ITEM: Explain how you divide 715 by 25 using your four-function pocket calculator.

CRITERION ITEM: Divide 715 by 25 using your four-function pocket calculator.

The audio directions are "Examine Mr. Shaeffer's two criterions items and select the one which more closely matches the objective."

As is evident from this example, the visual acts as the dominant component at this particular point, drawing the trainee's attention to a realistic situation where he or she would normally scan test items visually for suitability.

In an attempt to operationally describe the audiovisual training module, the emphasis to date has been on isolating and clarifying how each of the module components operates and contributes to learning. Putting all of them together, as has been implied all the way through, is what makes the design an effective one. The audiotape tells the students what to do. The visuals show them how it can be done. The response book lets them do it. There is no better means of expressing this interdependent relationship than by illustration. Examine the following script with accompanying visuals. Notice how each supports the other—all ultimately leading to the criterion item in the response book. This AV module is on "grid-drawings":

---

1. Shot of a ruler, a pencil, a small picture from a birthday card, and a large piece of drawing paper.

Sylvia: Is it difficult? Do you need special tools?
John: No, not at all. Even the cave man used it. And all you need is a ruler, a straight edge and a pencil. Let me demonstrate this process for you.

---

2. Closeup photograph of the picture on the birthday card with a 10 x 10 grid pattern drawn over it. The caption STEP 1 is superimposed on top.

Step 1, divide the original drawing into a large number of small squares. You do this by placing a grid pattern over it like this.

---

3. The large piece of drawing paper divided into a 10 x 10 grid. STEP 2 is superimposed.

Step 2, make a larger grid on another sheet of paper where you want your enlarged picture. You make this grid as big as your final picture should be.

---

4. Larger grid with the picture half done. Smaller picture on top with the grid pattern clearly visible. Superimposed caption: STEP 3.

Now that your drawing is broken up into little boxes, you can concentrate on copying one little section at a time. This is what you do in step 3.

---

5. Smaller picture and the completed enlargement. Faint grid lines are visible in both.

With a little practice you can even copy the most complex figure. Here's what the finished product looks like.

---

6. Medium shot of Sylvia drawing the last line of a grid over a picture from a torn page of a magazine.	*Sylvia: Okay let me see what I'm supposed to do. I'm a bit nervous. First I lay out a grid pattern over the original drawing.*
7. Sylvia completing a larger grid on a poster board.	*Next I make a larger grid.*
8. Sylvia copying one of the final cells in her enlarged drawing.	*Finally I copy the picture one small box at a time. But one thing worries me, though. What if the picture is in a book? I can't draw lines on it.*
9. Close up of John's hand placing a small piece of acetate with a grid over a picture in a basal reader.	*John: I'm glad you asked. In that case draw a grid on clear acetate—the stuff you use for overhead transparencies—or thin tracing paper and lay in on the picture.*
10. Caption: PLEASE TURN TO PAGE 12.	*Narrator: Sylvia is getting to practice her grid enlargement. Why don't you try to enlarge the same picture yourself. On page 12 of your response book you will find all the instructions for doing this. Turn off the tape and do this exercise. Best of luck in your artistic endeavors!*

The total effect, as you can see, is a tight combination of all components focusing in on one specific competency to be acquired by the student. He or she is directed by the audio, shown by means of the visuals, and then provided with an opportunity to demonstrate competence via the response book.

As we have been looking at excerpts from audiovisual training modules, a picture of how this design unites a number of instructional techniques through the various components should have emerged. The point of view which has been adopted so far has primarily been that of the teacher. When a trainee interacts with such a module, however, what does he or she see? How does the instructional content "flow into" the learner?

The audiovisual training module places the "burden" of learning squarely upon the learner. Module titles are usually in terms of the consumer: e.g., *Using Filters for Better Photography; More Effective Letter Writing; Use Your Calculator Wisely and Well;* or *Communicate through Graphics.* This lets the trainee know that as a result of using the module, he or she will become a more effective letter writer or be able to use his or her calculator wisely and well. The point here is that instruction becomes a pact between trainee and material. The instructor is left out of the contract. The responsibility for acquiring new competencies rests where it should be—with the trainee. This is reinforced by the audiovisual training module's objectives. Here are a series of objectives taken from a module on performing a task analysis:

General Objectives:

1. SPECIFY a main task appropriate for undergoing task analysis.
2. IDENTIFY subtasks at the preceding level of difficulty.
3. TREAT each subtask as a main task and identify simpler tasks at preceding levels of difficulty.
4. TERMINATE the analysis when a subtask reaches the pupils' entry level.
5. CONVERT a task analysis into a learning sequence.

Notice that everything is in terms of the learner and that all are demonstrable skills.

Once the trainee begins the AV module, the rest of the world disappears. A most interesting phenomenon is that in an individualized setting, with earphones on, the world gets cut out. The trainee's attention is rivetted to the problems at hand. Sight and sound are narrowed to the module presentation. Since the content of both the audio and visual concentrates on specific competencies which the *trainee must demonstrate* almost immediately, the trainee's mind cannot wander, as in a large lecture hall or even in a classroom. Everything extraneous is forced aside by audiovisual training module delivery.

As the trainee progresses through the module, copious examples are given and principles extracted. These examples are provided meaning and character through the wedding of audio with visual.

In an audiovisual training module, the trainee is introduced to a topic, provided with a series of problems, and then given training in preparing solutions along the way. Once the groundwork is laid, new problems are presented, and the trainee has to make responses while the number of prompts are diminished. Finally he or she is directed to the response book to demonstate his/her capacity to perform. Here is an example from the calculator module:

> How can we now find out how much sales tax you will have to pay on something you buy. Suppose a baseball costs $2.75. Press 2, point, 7, 5 and +. Now, how much is the sales tax in your area? Suppose it's 4%. Press 4 and then your % key. Your display should show this. That's your tax. Now press =. That's the total you would have to pay for the ball. Two dollars and seventy-five cents plus eleven cents sales tax is $2.86. Let's try another problem. This bicycle costs $59.95. You have sixty-three dollars exactly. Can you buy it? To calculate,

what do you do first? (Pause) Press 5, 9, point, 9, 5, and +. Let's say the sales tax is 5%. What do you do now? (Pause) Press 5, %, and =. (Pause) Your display should look like this. As we have already discussed when dealing with money, such a display means $62.95. This means you can buy your bicycle and have a nickel left over to start saving again. Do you think you are ready to try some problems on your own? Turn to page 9 of your response book. Try these problems. Turn off the tape until you are ready to go on.

HOW MUCH DO YOU ACTUALLY PAY?

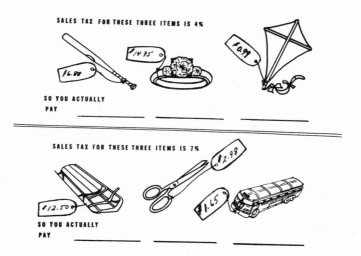

SALES TAX FOR THESE THREE ITEMS IS 4%

SO YOU ACTUALLY PAY ___ ___ ___

SALES TAX FOR THESE THREE ITEMS IS 7%

SO YOU ACTUALLY PAY ___ ___ ___

Turn on the tape when you have finished to check your calculations and your answers.

The response book also contains shorthand reminders of key calculation steps which the student can keep as a permanent performance aid and handy reference long after he or she has left the audiovisual training module behind.

To summarize, then, this chapter has provided an operational description of an audiovisual training module. There are three parts: visuals, an audiotape, and a response book. All parts make up a greater whole than a simple sum of what each contributes to the total design. Audiovisual training modules focus on specific competencies which can be demonstrated by a student. Every module contains performance objectives which are derived from careful analysis of the desired competency. For the teacher, the package contains criterion items, narrated and visualized instruction, and relevant references which can be delivered in a self-paced individualized curriculum. For the trainee, it is a means of getting instruction at the optimal time, hearing and seeing how something is done, getting a chance to do it, and then receiving immediate feedback through eyes and ears.

III.

DESIGN FORMAT

In this chapter, we discuss the various elements of the audiovisual training module design. We have already identified the three major components of this design: response book, audiotape, and slides (or filmstrip). Let's now examine what precisely is contained in each of these components. As we proceed through this chapter, you will encounter a number of examples to illustrate the function of each element of the audiovisual module.

The Response Book

The response book is the most important component of this design format. It is the part that provides the trainee with opportunities to respond, demonstrate, and try out newly acquired competencies. It also acts as the source for future reference after instruction.

The major elements of the response book are:

1. A statement of instructional objectives
2. Criterion items
3. Performance aids
4. References
5. Follow-up exercises
6. Glossary

Each of these elements is discussed below.

Objectives

The objectives of the module, both the general and specific ones, should be clearly stated near the beginning of the response book. The objectives should be derived from an analysis of the instructional task for the audiovisual training module. Here, for example, is an analysis of the task of producing an audiovisual training module:

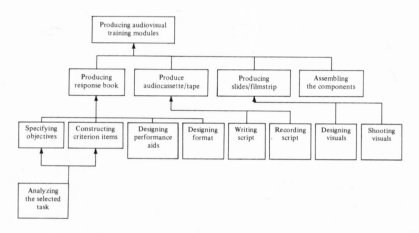

From this task analysis, the following set of objectives is derived. Notice the one-to-one correspondence between the objectives and the subtasks.

Objectives

Upon completion of this module, you will be able to produce your own audiovisual training module. Specifically, you will be able to demonstrate the following competencies:

1. SELECT a topic which is appropriate to your trainees and ANALYZE the task(s) implied in this topic.
2. SPECIFY a set of behavioral objectives for your audiovisual module based on your task analysis.
3. CONSTRUCT criterion items to match each objective of the audiovisual module.
4. DESIGN other content to be included in the response book.
5. DESIGN a suitable format for the response book.

6. WRITE a script which teaches toward each criterion item in the response book.
7. RECORD the audiotape for the module.
8. SPECIFY visuals to accompany the script.
9. SHOOT a set of slides for the audiovisual module.
10. ASSEMBLE all components of the audiovisual module.

The objectives should be clearly stated to indicate to the trainees exactly what skills they will acquire through their use of the module. Standards and conditions need not be included in the objectives unless they are essential to the content.

Criterion Items

Criterion items form the central core of the response book. These items are generated directly from the instructional objectives to measure whether or not a trainee has attained each objective. The audiovisual module is concerned with the acquisition of competencies. Therefore, the criterion items are concerned only with demonstrated performance. As an example, in an audiovisual training module on designing tutoring materials, this was the first objective:

SELECT a suitable skill to be taught through tutoring materials.

Here is the matching criterion item found in the response book.

What skill are you going to teach with your tutoring material? Describe it briefly here.

_____

_____

_____

The item asks the trainee directly to select and describe the skill he/she has chosen. Continuing with this same module, here is the second objective:

OUTLINE a tutoring lesson on the selected skill.

The designer of the module wrote the following two items for his response book:

1. What things should you do in preparing an outline for a tutoring lesson?

2. Prepare an outline for your tutoring material by:
   a. Writing down the specific objective.
   b. Specifying the format at different levels of difficulty.

Since the first item merely asked trainees to "talk about" the outline rather than actually do one, it was rejected. The second item, which required the performance specified in the objective, was incorporated into the response book.

Returning to the module on how to prepare audiovisual training modules, here are two sample criterion items from the response book. The objectives are also given to illustrate their correspondence to the items.

Objective 3: CONSTRUCT criterion items to match each objective of the audiovisual module. VERIFY the appropriateness of the criterion items using a given checklist.

Response book item: Construct a criterion item to perfectly match each objective. As you write each item, verify it against the checklist given below. A "no" answer to any question on the checklist means that you *must* rewrite your criterion item until you can answer "yes."

Checklist for Matching Objectives with Criterion Items

	YES	NO
1. Does the item require the same performance stated in the objective?	( )	( )

2. Is the main intent of the item the same as that of
the objective?   (   )   (   )

3. Is the trainee performance required in the item
directly observable and measurable?   (   )   (   )

4. Is the type of item (e.g., multiple choice, fill in the
blanks, application) the most appropriate one for
measuring attainment of the objective?   (   )   (   )

> When you have checked all your criterion items and can
> answer "yes" to every question on the checklist, please
> return to the audiotape.

Performance Aids

Since the response book serves as the "permanent" record of the audiovisual module and is retained by the trainee for later reference, it contains a number of performance aids to help the trainee when he is back "on-the-job." The performance aids act as prompting and assisting devices for transferring to the real world skills which are practiced during interaction with the module. The types of performance aids typically found in a response book include checklists, decision tables, information maps, charts, and figures.

Checklists. A checklist for verifying criterion items was shown earlier as an example. A checklist is a simple set of questions for which the answer is either "yes" or "no." In some situations, intermediate categories can be included. Generally, a product is considered acceptable if all of the items on a checklist are answered either by "yes" or with a checkmark. This type of performance aid helps the trainee decide if he has performed the task correctly. Here is another example of a checklist from a module on the wiring of circuit boards designed to assist the trainee to correctly select and wire a specified resistor into a given circuit board.

Wiring Checklist #7

	YES	NO
1. Does the resistor have the specified resistance?	( )	( )
2. Is the resistor correctly positioned in the circuit board?	( )	( )
3. Are soldered connections within the specified tolerances?	( )	( )
4. When connected to a battery and an ammeter, does the latter indicate a current flow of 15 amps?	( )	( )

A module on letter writing offers this sample checklist for evaluating a letter written to a client

Letter Checklist:
Setting up a Meeting with a Client

	YES	NO
1. Is the tone of your letter friendly and interested?	( )	( )
2. Does the letter come to the point quickly?	( )	( )
3. Are several alternative meeting times offered?	( )	( )
4. Does the letter end on a positive note of looking forward to the meeting?	( )	( )
5. Is it clear who wrote the letter?	( )	( )
6. Is it clear how and when the client can contact you?	( )	( )

A "no" to any question indicates
the need for revision.

Decision tables. A decision table essentially assists the trainee in making up his mind swiftly by identifying the variables and then reading the solution off a table. Following is a simple decision table included in the response book for a module for warehouse employees of a trucking firm. Notice how the table directs an employee rapidly to the correct phone number in case of an emergency.

	Number to Call in an Emergency (For two-digit numbers use INTERCOM) Call this number:		
If this happens:	*Day Shift*	*Evening Shift*	*Night Shift*
Accident	72	72	486-4111
Breakage	27	27	44
Fight	30	39	44
Fire	339-6000	339-6000	44
Mechanical trouble	29	428-6395	428-6395
Plumbing breakdown	36	40	491-7830
Power failure	36	40	332-2849
Sickness	72	72	486-4111
Theft	30	30	44
Any other emergency	44	44	44

Information maps. A concise and effective method for presenting a large amount of information in a clear fashion is through the use of information maps. Similar to a table, it condenses long narrative passages into succinct blocks of information which are organized for easy access. A sample of the way the information mapping approach can be utilized in a response book is taken again from our module on producing audiovisual modules. Here, the response book offers information mapped summaries on the various stages of evaluation a module should undergo during development. This particular sample is on group testing a module.

STAGE 4. *Group Testing*

WHY?

Formative purpose: To identify recurrent error patterns in student responses and make appropriate modifications.

Summative purpose: To obtain student-performance data on the effects of the audiovisual training module.

WHO?

Developer.

Groups of target students.

WHEN?

After individual tryouts produce consistent and satisfactory results.

WHAT?

The audiovisual training module in its latest revised form.

Adjunct material: Complete set of instructions to the student.

Measuring instruments: Criterion-referenced tests based on the instructional objectives, entry tests based on the list of prerequisite skills, and observation checklists for collecting process data.

HOW?

1. Administer the entry test to the students before they receive the module.

2. Distribute the copies of the module to the students and explain how to use them.

3. Let the students work on their own. Collect observation data on the students' use of the module.

4. Administer the criterion-referenced test immediately after each student completes working through the module.

5. Tabulate test performance results for each student on each item. Examine the table for patterns of errors. Make suitable modifications in the module.

6. Compare error patterns with entry test performance to check your assumptions about target students. To compensate for the lack

of any prerequisite skills, develop remediation supplements where applicable.

7. Retest with a new group of students if major modifications have to be made.

Flowcharts. An excellent means of summarizing a long, detailed procedure for trainees to follow at a later time is a flowchart. Flowcharts permit the trainee to visually trace the steps in a procedure. The steps are written in rectangular boxes. Whenever there is a decision point, a "yes-no"question is written inside a diamond. All the boxes and diamonds have lines with arrows emanating from them showing the trainee where to go next. In an audiovisual training module on tutoring handicapped children, a series of flowcharts in the response book clearly lay out the procedures to be used with various tutoring materials. Figure 1 illustrates the procedure for a simple addition exercise.

Tables. Tables that summarize information presented in the other components of the module make excellent performance aids for trainees. Very often, the audiotape describes technical processes and the appropriate circumstances for instituting them. This information may be too concentrated for the trainee to retain. For easy reference in the future, this information may be conveniently packaged within the response book. A table can compact a lot of information into a small area.

Returning to our module on producing audiovisual modules, Table 1 is a table comparing a number of duplicating processes along five dimensions.

Figure 1

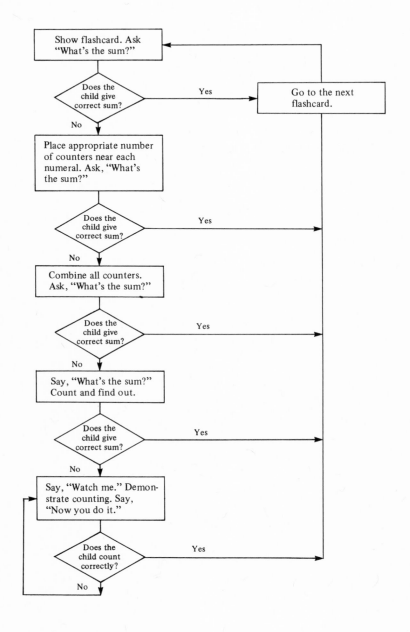

Table 1

Comparison Table of Duplicating Processes

PROCESS	COST	NO. OF COPIES	COMPLEXITY	TURN AROUND TIME	QUALITY
Spirit	Very cheap about 20¢ per stencil and ½¢ per duplicated page.	Approximately 30 per stencil	Simple to run	30 copies per page requires about 5 minutes.	Some color, but not usually slick.
Stencil (Mimeo)	Fairly cheap. About 45¢ per stencil and ¾¢ per page.	Approximately 200 good copies per stencil.	Moderately simple to do. Somewhat messy If you've never tried it you'll need help.	200 copies per page requires about 10 minutes.	Print looks clean and drawings come out well, but color is a pretty big problem.
Xerox IBM Olivetti, etc.	About 5¢ per page.	Any number	Very simple.	100 copies requires about 10 minutes.	Gives an excellent reproduction of the original, but no color.
Offset	High for small quantities but gets cheaper with volume.	Any number.	You need a pro.	You have to get in line— usually a couple of days.	The best. You can reproduce photos and all the color you want. But it's expensive!

References

The response book is intimately related to the audio and visual portions of the module, all forming the "leanest" possible instructional vehicle for leading the trainees toward the attainment of the specified objectives. To amplify and supplement the contents of the module, a set of references should be included. This should contain both a bibliography of print materials and a "mediagraphy" of such nonprint resources as films, videotapes, records, games, tapes, computer assisted instruction programs, slides, and other audio-visual modules. These references should be limited to relevant and useful items. Each entry should be annotated with a brief indication of the contents.

Follow-up Exercises

Once the trainee completes the audiovisual module, he or she may be given some follow-up activities beyond the audio-visual portions. These activities are primarily designed to promote transfer of the acquired skills to simulated or real contexts. These follow-up activities serve to complete the process of acquiring a relevant competency. To illustrate, here is an example, from an audiovisual module for training preservice teachers on a form of classroom questioning called "personalized question." This example forms the follow-up activity suggested in the response book:

Microteaching Exercise

Locate a few friends who have gone through this module and are willing to participate in a roleplay situation with you. Select one trainee to teach a five-minute lesson based on the following story. The other trainees play the roles of third graders. Use personalized questions whenever appropriate. During the lesson one member of your group should act as an observer, using the checklist on page 11. After the lesson, use the information recorded on this checklist as a basis for discussion. It is a good idea to repeat this experience, switching roles and objectives.

Checklist for the Observer

While one of your peers teaches the lesson, carefully observe his/her use of personalized questions. Use the following checklist for recording your observations:

1. Number of personalized questions used:

2. Number of inappropriate personalized questions:

3. Number of times the teacher was distracted into tangential discussions:

4. Were the personalized questions distributed among all the students?
( ) yes
( ) somewhat
( ) no

Glossary

A glossary is a welcome addition to the response book. At the beginning of the response book, the trainees should be informed about the availability of this glossary. The first time a technical term is used in the response book it is marked with an asterisk to signal that an explanation can be found in the glossary.

Section Summary

The response book is the key component of the audiovisual training module. It is also the trainee's personal link to the instructional content after the audiovisual components have been completed. The response book is brief and functionally organized both for initial learning and future reference. All response books contain a statement of objectives and criterion items. In addition, depending upon the content of the module, it may contain various performance aids, references, follow-up exercises, and a glossary.

The Audiotape

The response book is the major learning component while the audiotape is the major teaching component of the audiovisual training module. The audiotape generally directs, explains, describes, encourages, and reinforces the trainee. This component may use various audio techniques, including music, dialogue, narration, interview, and sound montage. However, all these techniques have one distinct purpose: to lead the trainee from his or her entry level to the criterion items in the response book in the most motivating and efficient way possible. The criterion items are laid out in sequence and a script is created to lead the trainee toward these items. One of the most effective means of doing this is to create a storyline with authentic characters and real-world problems. In an audiovisual module on using the pocket calculator, fifth grade children are shown using their calculators to work on problems any child might face: How much money will be saved by Christmas? How much wood is needed to build a birdhouse? School children using the module are encouraged to participate in finding solutions to the problems that confront the characters in the module. An audiovisual module on producing audiovisual training modules uses a story about a trainer with an instructional problem who produces his own module.

To illustrate the approach to the production of motivating and instructionally effective audiotapes, let us examine one that uses all of the audio techniques mentioned earlier. This sample audiotape is from a module entitled *Parents as Partners*. Its overall objective is to help the teacher design and implement a program which enables parents to actively participate in the teaching of their children. The audiotape is divided into seven parts: teaser, preliminaries, summary of objectives, content, references to the response book, conclusion, and follow-up activities. What follows is a description of each of these parts in terms of its function, purpose, time allotment, and style.

The teaser. Getting into a module, sitting down, and focusing attention to the task at hand usually requires several minutes. To speed up the process, a teaser can be used. The teaser is a brief dramatic episode that orients the trainee to the context and provides a preview of a problem. It is a dramatic form of advanced organizer. Just as in a television show, the audiovisual module can use this teaser opening to catch the attention of the viewer, and pull his or her thoughts toward the instructional topic. Thrown into the middle of some critical event, the trainee quickly becomes an active participant. Since the idea of a teaser is to capture the attention of the trainee, and get into instruction as quickly as possible, it should be very brief, lasting no more than 30 to 45 seconds. In *Parents as Partners*, the audiotape begins with the dialing of a telephone followed by a brief conversation. Sound effects, a telephone microphone, and dialogue are used to enhance realism. The young teacher, Mrs. Merton, is someone with whom trainees can readily identify.

(Sound of dialing ... and ringing tone in receiver.)

(Mrs. Merton thinking to herself) "I hope they're home ... there's really no other way to go about it ... Gwen simply needs more help with her reading and math ... and all the attention she can get ... I'm sure Mrs. Davis can help her child in all these ways if only I can convince her to do it ... I hear she's very concerned ..."

(Voice answers) "Hello?"

Mrs. Merton: "Hello, Mrs. Davis?"

Mrs. Davis: "Yes?"

Mrs. Merton: "Oh good! This is Caroline Merton, Gwen's teacher."

Mrs. Davis: "Oh yes, Mrs. Merton. What can I do for you? Is there any problem?"

Mrs. Merton: "Oh no, nothing like that. You see, Gwen's really doing fine. ..." (Music up and over as voice fades.)

Preliminaries. Once the trainee's attention has been focused through the teaser, the audiotape identifies the module by title. There are some procedural mechanics to be dealt with, such as identifying the components and directing the trainee on how to use them and stating the rationale for the module. This leads the trainee to check whether he or she is on the right module and has all the necessary pieces. This part should be brief—not more than a few seconds—and delivered in a businesslike style. Here is how *Parents as Partners* does it:

Welcome to PARENTS AS PARTNERS. In the module we'll be dealing with effective ways for getting parents to help teach their own children.

The module consists of a filmstrip and a response book in addition to the audiotape you are listening to now. Please make sure that the filmstrip is on the title frame now. Also make sure that you have your personal copy of the response booklet. If there are any problems, stop the tape now and call your instructor.

I'm sure you've heard some of your colleagues recount their experiences in using parents to help their own children with schoolwork or other related learning activities. Some may have had good experiences; others may have had only negative things to relate. But there is one overwhelming fact for you to remember: The pupils in your classroom are influenced every day by what happens both at school and in the home. Teachers and parents *working together* can build the consistent learning environment which is so important for children. General experience as well as research clearly indicates that parents working as partners with teachers offers powerful advantages to the child, to the teacher, to learning. This is what this module is about.

Summary of objectives. Following the preliminaries, it is generally a good idea to briefly present and comment on the objectives of the training module. This acquaints the trainee with the competencies he or she will be acquiring. This brief presentation offers a rationale for the objectives and acts as an advanced organizer to the entire module. It generally takes no longer than a minute. *Parents as Partners* offers an example of such a narrative summary of objectives:

Please open the booklet now and turn to pages 1 and 2 for the objectives of this module. When you hear the tone turn off the tape recorder and take a minute to look over these objectives. After you have done this, turn the tape back on. (Signal tone. Pause.)

As the objectives in the response book informed you, this module will provide you with skills and techniques you can use in establishing a program that enables parents to actively participate in teaching their youngsters. By the time you complete this module, you will have prepared arguments for convincing parents to become partners in their children's education. You will also have planned ways of contacting parents and interviewing them, designed training sessions, identified materials for parent use, and provided means for maintaining your parent-tutoring program.

The content. The bulk of the audiotape is concerned with the instructional content of the module. Ideally, the running time for the audio should be between 15 and 30 minutes. A period longer than 30 minutes is usually too overwhelming for the trainee. Using narration, dialogue, examples, and explanations, the tape guides the trainee to the point at which he or she is ready to respond to a criterion item. To illustrate how the tape does this, let us examine a segment from *Parents as Partners.* Notice how the trainee is smoothly led to the criterion items in the response book.

Although the phone is the most practical means of contacting parents, it is not always the best or even a possible way. In some cases, the family may not have a phone. Parents whose native language isn't English may not understand you over the phone or be able to respond quickly.

A letter may turn out to be your surest means of communication in these cases. If you know that the parent you wish to contact is at work when you want to call, again, a letter is your best solution.

Almost the same rules apply to the letter as to the telephone call: Make it friendly and interested, come to the point clearly and quickly, offer several possible meeting times, and end on a positive note. Two additional considerations are important: let the parents know exactly who you are and how they can contact you. Remember, a parent with several children might not recall who you are. A contact by letter should include your address and phone number as well as the time periods when you can be reached.

Please turn to page 6 of your response booklet. There is a little letter-writing assignment on this page which asks you to play the role of Mrs. Merton. You have failed to reach Mrs. Davis over the phone. Your task is to write Mrs. Davis a letter incorporating the suggestions we gave you earlier. Turn off the tape recorder while you work on this assignment. (Signal tone)

* * *

Since we cannot see your letter, you have to evaluate it yourself. Please turn to the next page of your response book for a checklist. Rate your letter by answering "yes" or "no" to each of the items on the checklist. You may find it convenient to tear off the page to make

the comparisons with your letter easier. Turn off the tape while you
undertake this self-evaluation. (Signal tone)

                              *   *   *

I hope your checklist has "yes" checked off beside each question.
Just remember that the only clue the parents have, when they don't
know you personally, is the initial letter. A good first impression will
pave the way for a successful partnership.

References to the response book. The response book contains criterion items, performance aids, and other materials.
As the audiotape leads the trainee through the module, it
refers him or her to the parts of the response book where
additional information is provided. Whenever print offers
itself as the best medium for delivering a message, the tape
may direct the trainee to the response book. It may also refer
to printed summaries of the instructional content. Here's
an example of the dialogue discussing the "do's" and
"don'ts" of parent-teacher conferences followed by a printed
summary. This lengthy example also illustrates the use of
dialogue for instructional presentations.

Now that the initial contact has been made, we have to consider
the first meeting. The primary aim of this meeting is to enlist the parents' support and active willingness to participate as partners in their
children's learning. This meeting should be as pleasant as possible. Let's
return to Mr. Roloff, the principal, and Mrs. Merton, who are now
discussing such a meeting.
    Mr. Roloff: You should have firmly fixed in your mind exactly
why the meeting is taking place. The overall objective of this confer-
ence is *to get the parents to become active partners in teaching their
child.* You want to learn something of the home environment and rela-
tionships which are important to Gwen's development. You should tell
Mrs. Davis something about Gwen's experiences at school and how she
is reacting to them. And from this exchange of information, you and
Mrs. Davis can develop a cooperative plan that you can work on together for Gwen's benefit both at home and at school.
    Mrs. Merton: How specific should this plan be?
    Mr. Roloff: I would recommend a very specific plan. Otherwise, Mrs.
Davis may have problems figuring out exactly what she is to do and
why she is doing it.

Mrs. Merton: How does this goal sound? Mrs. Davis is to administer exercises and play some learning games to raise Gwen's math scores to at least 70%.

Mr. Roloff: You're a quick learner. You're really on the track now. Vague promises don't help much at all. On the other hand, don't promise what you can't deliver.

Mrs. Merton: How about preparing the parents and giving them specific materials?

Mr. Roloff: Hold on. That comes later. At this meeting you may want to show Mrs. Davis some sample materials to point out that there is nothing terribly complicated in what you are asking of them.

Mrs. Merton: Okay. Once they're convinced, then I guess I invite them to a training session.

Mr. Roloff: Right. We should talk about those, too, but first I think it would be a good idea to go over some of the very basic but important rules about parent-teacher conferences—and these go for parent-teacher conferences held for any reason—and especially when the parents involved have handicapped children.

Mrs. Merton: Well, right away I can think of things like beginning with a positive statement about the child's capabilities or interests.

Mr. Roloff: Right. That'll make parents less defensive and show them that you really like their child. Also, comparing observations about how the child acts or responds at home and at school can offer some useful insights for both parents and you.

But keep in mind that when you talk about the child's action, parents sometimes may take this as a criticism of themselves.

Mrs. Merton: That means that, as a teacher, I should listen to complaints about the school or myself without getting upset, too.

Mr. Roloff: Yes, because sometimes parental comments will offer valuable clues or suggestions which you can use.

Mrs. Merton: Well, I've collected a useful list of "do's." Now how about telling me some of the "don'ts?"

Mr. Roloff: Well, in some ways, that's easier. First, don't make comparisons between pupils in the classroom. It only causes bad feelings and takes you away from the subject at hand. Another thing, don't criticize past teachers or schools. The present and the future should be the focus of attention. And while I'm thinking of it, don't suggest that the parents are to blame for the child's difficulties. You'll lose any good feelings they may have if you put them on the defensive. Finally, don't give advice unless asked for, and even then not as a foolproof answer.

Armed with these suggestions for "do's" and "don'ts," Caroline Merton has made a list of what she should remember. It is reproduced on page 8 of your response booklet. You may find this checklist useful for you when you schedule your first parent-teacher meeting.

Conclusion. The conclusion of the audiotape is almost as important as the opening teaser. The teaser attempted to fade out the real world and lead the trainee into the core of the module to gather new competencies. The trainee has shared a number of experiences with the characters of the module. The conclusion returns the trainee to the real world where he or she must apply these freshly acquired skills. This closing part of the audiotape summarizes the content and the objectives of the module, encourages the trainee to use what has been learned, and offers action suggestions for immediate application. The conclusion should be short and optimistic as in this sample segment from *Parents as Partners.*

This module has encouraged you to use parents as partners to help the children in your classroom learn better. Parents are the strongest resource the child has for learning outside the school. By going through this module, you have prepared a plan for enlisting their aid. Let's now leave as we came in. Remember Mrs. Merton's phone call?

Mrs. Merton: (fading in) "No, Mrs. Davis, there certainly is no problem with Gwen. The reason I'm calling is to discuss some ways you and Mr. Davis and I can help Gwen do even better. You see, I feel ..."

Good luck, Mrs. Merton, in your parents-as-partners plan.

Follow up activities. Some modules may include on the audiotape suggested follow-up activities as part of the concluding remarks. These may consist of application exercises, practice exercises, simulation and roleplay activities, and larger project and small-group discussion sessions. The following table shows examples of each of these from various audiovisual modules.

Module	Type of Activity	Actual Follow-up Activity
Observing and Recording an Animal's Behavior	Application exercise	Select the animal you are going to observe. Set up your observation schedule. Note the animal's behavior over the next five days at the times you have selected.
The Orchestra	Practice exercise	Use the exercise cassette to sharpen your recognition skills. Turn on the tape and listen to the instruments. In your response book pages 14 to 36 you have a series of practice exercises. Follow the directions, listen to the tape, and select the correct answer to each question.
Personalized Questions	Simulation/roleplay	Locate several friends who have gone through this module. Select one person to be the teacher. All others play the role of third graders. Teach a five-minute lesson to them on the following story ...
Producing Audiovisual Training Modules	Large project requiring application of all the skills	Prepare your own audiovisual module on a suitable topic.

As an example of the discussion type of follow-up activity, let us conclude by examining the final remarks from the audiotape from *Parents as Partners*.

This concludes the module on parents as partners. Of course, we haven't said everything there is to say about this topic. There are many aspects which we have not been able to bring out. For example, we did not discuss problems faced by working parents, parents of large families, or single parents. Non-English speaking families and different ethnic groups pose special problems. Another new question involves the legal rights of parents and children in regard to test results and school information. How much must the parents be told?

Many of these complex and controversial issues are listed on the last page of the response booklet. Rather than imposing our points of view on these issues, we would like to suggest that you discuss them with your friends. As a final assignment, we would like you to gather some of your colleagues, especially those who have gone through this module, and spend about thirty minutes in a small-group session discussing these issues ... (Music up.)

Section Summary

The audiotape carries the major instructional burden. It contains music, narration, dialogue, sound effects, and directions. While audiotapes can be single-voice narrations, the more varied the techniques (without adding variety for its own sake) the more likely it is that the audio message will make an impact. A brief teaser to capture the trainee's attention, preliminaries, overview of the objectives, instructional content, references to the response book, conclusion, and follow-up exercises can all be included in the audiotape. No audiotape, no matter how interesting, can be expected to hold the learner's attention longer than 30 minutes.

The Slides/Filmstrip

Accompanying the audiotape and sometimes assuming the main instructional burden is the set of visuals for the audiovisual training module. Just as the audiotape leads the trainee toward each criterion item of the response book through narration and sound effects, the slides lead the trainee to the same goal using a variety of visual messages. The audiotape cuts out the extraneous noise to focus the trainee's attention. The visuals cut out the extraneous sights to build a new temporary environment for the trainee. The audio and visual components are closely intertwined and these are designed almost simultaneously, despite the order in which they are discussed in this chapter. Sometimes the visuals evolve from the audioscript; at other times they generate the narrative.

Functions of the Visuals

In general, the visuals on the slides or filmstrips serve six different functions:

1. *Environment.* The visuals provide the real-life context in which the skills are to be applied.

2. *Enhancements.* In teaching a procedural task, the visuals "show" while the audiotape "tells" each of the steps during the demonstration of the skilled performance.

3. *Examples.* In teaching a concept or principle, the visuals provide a divergent set of examples.

4. *Instructions.* The visuals summarize directions given on the tape to ensure that the trainee follows them.

5. *Summary.* The visuals provide summaries of the principles and procedures taught in the module.

6. *Enrichment.* The visuals utilize logical opportunities to go beyond the specific instructional objectives of the module without interfering with its essential focus.

Each of these functions of the visuals is described and illustrated below:

The Visuals Provide an Environment

It is an ordinary night along highway 62. A big eighteen wheeler is moving along at the speed limit right on schedule. A bit of fog is drifting in over this lonely stretch of road. Suddenly, there is a sharp jolt and the truck lurches right ...

This is the introduction to an audiovisual module about emergencies on the road for interstate-driver trainees. As the audio provides the sound effects for the introduction, a series of slides pass before the trainee's eyes: A steering wheel and darkness with a highway sign with the number 62 reflecting the truck's headlights; a mile marker passing by the window, the schedule on the dash shows the time and mileage. The clock shows the same time. Another slide appears showing the lights cutting the light fog. As the sound of the jolts and bumps of a truck lurching out of control hit the trainee's ears, a slide shows the truck cab askew. Another slide appears with the driver's foot on the brake with a big red "X" over it.

This set of slides presents the context for the module on trucking emergencies. The trainee views a series of visual clues so that she or he can immediately perceive what is going on. The red "X" over the foot on the brake tells him the driver has done something wrong. Throughout this segment, not a word is spoken. This sample segment illustrates how visuals can transport the trainee to the real-life environment.

The Visuals Provide Enhancement

The audiotape says to the art student: *Let me demonstrate this process for you. Step 1, divide the original drawing into a number of small squares by pacing a grid pattern over it like this. Step 2, make a larger grid on another sheet of paper where you want your enlarged picture. You make this grid as big as your final picture should be. Now that your drawing is broken up into little boxes, you can concentrate on copying one little section at a time. This is what you do ...*

Without some form of visual representation, the steps given by the narrator would most likely convey little meaning to the trainee. However, this explanation is accompanied by slides or filmstrips. In terms of trying to model the same procedure, the trainee now has a picture of what must be done in order to use the grid technique for enlargement.

The Visuals Illustrate by Example

The visual part of the audiovisual training module can illustrate a concept or a principle by a number of realistic examples. An audiovisual training module on traffic safety tells about the many hazards in the streets, then backs it up with a long series of visuals showing potential accident spots. Slides show children crossing between cars, riding bicycles in traffic, crossing on a red light, climbing a railway crossing barrier, and chasing a ball onto the road.

Another module, on analyzing paintings, illustrates by a multitude of examples the differences between simple, complex, repeated, and spaced use of lines across art forms. An architecture trainee views a segment of an audiovisual training module illustrating the broad range of applications of the cantilever to a variety of structures around the world.

The Visuals Give Instructions

The audiotape generally directs the attention of the trainee and tells him/her when to turn off the tape, turn to a certain page of the response book, or go out and practice a skill. Since the auditory message is fleeting, visual accompaniment in the form of a redundant set of directions increases the likelihood of the directions being followed. In most audiovisual modules, it is good practice to include a slide with the page number to which the trainee is to turn. These instructions can be provided in imaginative ways to avoid a mechanical appearance. In one module on sports, each time the trainee is sent to the response book, the caption "Turn to page ..." is superimposed on a live photograph of a sporting person whose sweater shows the page number. In another module on traffic safety, the "stop-the-tape" directions appear on a stop sign, while the "Go to page ..." is superimposed over a green light.

The Visuals Provide a Summary

In a procedural task, a visual summary of the steps helps the trainee synthesize what has been described earlier. One design technique for building effective summaries is through successive disclosure. A series of slides, one after another, reviews the main points, adding more and more to the whole, the latest addition highlighted in a brighter color. The total effect is to reinforce the essential points the module is making. To illustrate the use of the visuals for a summary, here is a segment from an audiovisual training module for instructional materials developers on designing games. This segment is the summary of the tryout and revision stage.

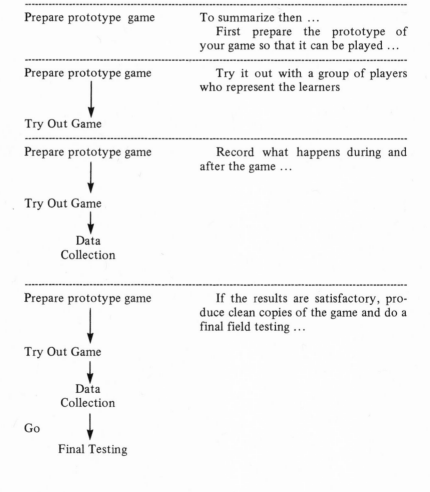

Prepare prototype game   To summarize then ...
                                First prepare the prototype of
                                your game so that it can be played ...

Prepare prototype game   Try it out with a group of players
                                     who represent the learners

Try Out Game

Prepare prototype game   Record what happens during and
                                after the game ...

Try Out Game

Data
Collection

Prepare prototype game   If the results are satisfactory, pro-
                                     duce clean copies of the game and do a
                                     final field testing ...

Try Out Game

Data
Collection

Go

Final Testing

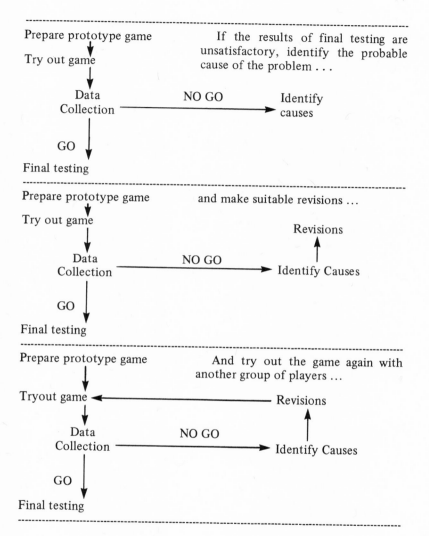

Another illustration of the visual summary with live photographs is from a module on developing black and white photographic prints. There, the summary contains a build up of items required for printing a photograph.

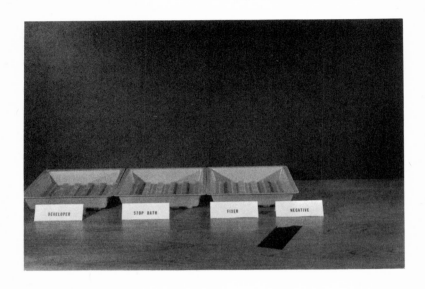

IV.

OUTCOMES

Audiovisual training modules offer a number of advantageous outcomes for attaining both complex objectives and objectives requiring transfer and applications. These outcomes provide benefits for trainees, instructors, and administrators.

The Audiovisual Training Module for Complex Objectives

The audiovisual training module is a flexible and effective design for assisting trainees to attain even the most difficult instructional objectives. It permits trainees to observe, practice, and utlimately acquire complex skills. For example, the audiovisual module on art techniques, which we earlier described, presents each step in the complex procedure for producing grid drawings through sight and sound. At the same time, as the trainee views each step, the audiotape explains how it is done and even encourages the trainee as he or she tries it himself/herself. The audiovisual training module can illustrate complex chains for starting up a computer or a printing press with slides that include close-ups of each switch and dial, while the audiotape delivers the appropriate sounds. Through the use of audiovisual modules, trainees can observe interview techniques, listen in on the interactions, and even evaluate interviewees with a checklist from the response book. Armed with their experiences from such modules, trainees can go out and practice complex skills acquired from the audiovisual training module in real or simulated situations with increased chances of success.

The Audiovisual Training Module
for Transfer and Application

Particularly where instructional objectives are geared to transfer and application, the audiovisual training module can be most effective. Instructional content such as solving equations, doing map reading, or analyzing sentences are readily handled by the single medium of print. Skills that involve a high degree of transfer, however, such as following safety regulations on the road, at home, and at school, storing perishable items, or using certain types of classroom questioning techniques with children, can be more accurately portrayed and more realistically delivered via the audiovisual module. What trainees gain from this form of instruction is a greater sense of realism than textbook and lecture can provide.

The Audiovisual Module and Individualization

Although audiovisual training modules are flexible enough to permit delivery in small- and large-group settings, essentially this format is for the individual. A trainee may select his or her module from the shelf, plug it in, and receive a competency-based unit of instruction requiring virtually no outside intervention. As more and more educational programs become individualized, the audiovisual training module becomes increasingly appropriate. The objectives are laid out for the trainee. Instruction is self-administered. Self-testing by means of the criterion items in the response book is also built into the design. As a trainee completes one module, he or she can be checked out by an instructor or monitor and allowed to proceed at his or her own rate to the next instructional phase. Through this type of individualized delivery, a trainee can follow an individually prescribed program with little need to worry about what "the others" are doing.

In summary, then, the audiovisual training module allows trainees to engage in self-instruction on self-selected topics following self-paced schedules and utilizing self-monitoring procedures to gauge their own competency acquisition.

The Audiovisual Training Module and the Trainee

For the trainee, the audiovisual module offers a form of instruction that directly meets his or her needs. The objectives are clearly presented. Instruction is restricted to the relevant. The audiovisual module is involving and is addressed directly to the trainee. The acquisition of competencies becomes the sole responsibility of the trainee who, through completing exercises in the response book and then verifying his or her responses from the feedback, can monitor his or her own progress. The audiovisual module permits the trainee to see what is being presented, to hear the explanation, to try it out personally, and then to correct his or her errors. Where a point has been missed, the trainee can review again and again a segment of the module and repeatedly re-test himself or herself.

Because the audiovisual training module shows realistic situations and uses characters with whom trainees can identify, instruction is meaningful and outcomes can be more readily transfered to real-life situations. The response book which the trainee keeps remains as a reference and resource as well as a reminder of instruction long after direct contact with instruction has been left behind. In summary, the audiovisual training module leaves the trainee with a set of skills which he or she has seen and heard being applied in a variety of situations and has even tried out in a restricted setting. These skills are now ready to be applied in the real world.

The Audiovisual Training Module and the Instructor

Instructors and teachers need as much time to plan lessons, prepare meaningful examples, design tests, and correct student work as they do to actually teach a unit. The audiovisual module, although initially requiring extensive development effort, once produced becomes a reusable form of instruction which can be shared with other instructors and which frees the instructor from a number of planning, teaching, testing, and correcting activities. The instructor is no longer the exclusive purveyor of information, but rather becomes a manager, troubleshooter, and guide. The instructor can focus on specific problems trainees experience rather than on the dispensing of information which an audiovisual module can more clearly and patiently convey. Freed from the chore of repeatedly describing mechanical procedures and skills or verbally explaining complex concepts, the instructor can concentrate on monitoring individual trainee progress and upon the transfer and application of competencies to real-life situations. The audiovisual module provides trainees with essential skills that can now be applied where needed. Instructors are thus freed from much of the drudgery of their jobs.

The Audiovisual Training Module and the Administrator

Once a curriculum has been developed and essential competencies have been specified, audiovisual training modules offer the administrator a means of assuring instruction of the specified skills. Compared with other multimedia forms of production, the audiovisual training module is inexpensive, yet it delivers with virtually the same impact. Administrators can easily verify trainee progress from records of module use.

Examples in keeping with specific on-the-job or out-in-the-world needs can be built into the modules. As changes in procedures, equipment, or knowledge occur, audiovisual modules can be revised. Since the audiovisual module can be used virtually anywhere, instructional space requirements are reduced, while equipment costs are kept relatively low.

Audiovisual modules require little more storage space than books. Reproduction costs are small. Trainees need minimal training to use an audiovisual module. Because of the reusable and self-instructional nature of the audiovisual training module, teachers and instructors can be assigned more time for assisting trainees with application tasks and for counseling. Thus, from the administrative point of view, the audiovisual training module provides an effective as well as efficient form of instruction, offering a wide variety of benefits for relatively low investments of time and money.

Dangers and Limitations of Audiovisual Training Modules

Although the audiovisual module affords a number of benefits to trainee, instructor, and administrator, it does possess several limitations. Since the stress is on individualized delivery, interaction among trainees is seriously reduced. The audiovisual module cuts the trainee off from others. Unless it specifically directs trainees to search out one another or to roleplay in a group, the trainee can become isolated from his peers.

Since the audiovisual module as described in this book contains only still visuals, skills which require motion or manipulation are best dealt with using other designs. Newer equipment, however, can speed up the presentation of slides or filmstrip frames to *simulate motion*. The precision required in the production phase, though, and the increased cost of equipment for trainees makes forcing the audiovisual training module format to accommodate motion less worthwhile than video or super-8 film.

One danger that arises in working with any medium is that it can become a fascinating end in itself with greater attention focused on the medium than on the message. The audiovisual training module attempts to bring the real world to the trainee through sight and sound. Although research has shown that there is little difference in learning outcomes between fairly crudely produced materials and "slick" products, producers tend to extend themselves to the fullest to obtain the most aesthetically pleasing result. Trainees do enjoy well produced materials, and instructors more readily try a neatly designed package, but a balance between the medium and message must be maintained. When too much attention and expense is placed on obtaining split screen images, clever cartoons or stereophonic and electrifying sound effects rather than on the *instructional effectiveness* of the module, the trainee becomes the loser.

One serious limitation to producing audiovisual training modules is the initial expense both of money and time that is required. Capital outlay is needed—for a good camera, lenses, a copystand, lights, lettering devices, audio equipment, and related supplies. Developing, recording, printing, and reproducing can be expensive. Instructors require release time to design modules. Technical help, even from trainees or other personnel, is also needed. From experience, the first module a developer attempts to produce generally requires a lot of time and numerous revisions before he or she is satisfied with the results. This can be discouraging for the novice testing out the audiovisual training module design.

Summary

Use of the audiovisual training module results in a number of desirable outcomes. It permits trainees to experience instruction which is realistic and meaningful. Because the audiovisual training module provides multi-channel instruction, trainees can acquire complex competencies rapidly. The design allows trainees to observe, to practice, and to correct themselves. Trainees, instructors, and administrators benefit from use of the audiovisual training module. It is an ideal vehicle for self-instruction. The limitations to the design are that it cannot readily handle objectives in which motion and manipulation are dominant; it can become aesthetically self-conscious to the detriment of instruction; and it requires relatively heavy initial investment of both money and time compared to traditional classroom instruction.

V.

DEVELOPMENTAL GUIDE

Over a period of years, we have devised a ten-step approach to producing audiovisual training modules. These steps have been formatively evaluated and modified in the production of over thirty training modules. The reader may find this systematic procedure useful in the production of his own audiovisual training module.

1. Perform a task analysis of your selected topic.
2. Convert subtasks to performance objectives.
3. Construct a criterion item to match each objective.
4. Write the script toward each criterion item.
5. Design a visual storyboard which specifies the content of the slides or filmstrip frames.
6. Design the response book.
7. Produce the response book.
8. Produce the audiotape.
9. Produce the slides.
10. Assemble the total module.

The following pages offer some details and examples for each of the steps.

---

1. Perform a task analysis of your selected topic.

WHY?

1. To systematically break the main task down into its prerequisite subtasks until the entry level of the trainee is reached.
2. To provide a base for deriving specific performance objectives for the modules.

WHEN?

1. Right at the outset as soon as a topic or a main task has been identified.

WHO?

1. The developer of the module and the subject matter expert(s). (In some cases this is the same person.)

WHAT?

1. At this stage paper and pencil or a chalk board are sufficient. Index cards may also be used.

HOW?

1. Specify your main task.
2. Identify all necessary substasks at the next simplest level.
3. Take each subtask and treat it as a main task, identifying the necessary prerequisite subtasks at the next simplest level.
4. Repeat this procedure at each level until the trainees' entry level has been reached.
5. Edit the task analysis to eliminate all superfluous subtasks which do not contribute to the main task. Add overlooked items. The task analysis should contain all necessary and sufficient subtasks to be complete.

Example:

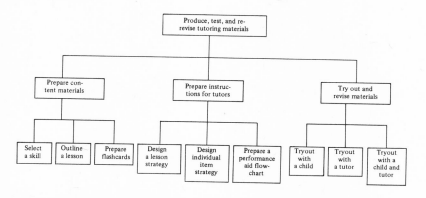

---

2. Convert subtasks to performance objectives.

WHY?

1. To inform the trainee in precise terms as to what s/he will accomplish as a result of working through the audiovisual training module.
2. To provide a base for deriving criterion items.

WHEN?

1. Once the task analysis has been completed and edited.

WHO?

1. Primarily the developer of the module. Once the objectives are written, the subject matter expert should verify them to ensure their validity.

WHAT?

1. Paper or index cards and pencil.

HOW?

1. Write an overall objective for the module which matches the main task.

2. For each subtask, prepare a matching objective. Each objective should contain a behavioral term which indicates overtly what the trainee will be able to accomplish. Unless the task requires it, standards and conditions need not be included.

3. Arrange the objectives in an instructional sequence so that the first thing the trainee will be able to do appears first.

4. Edit the objectives so that they form a coherent and logically sequenced set. Eliminate redundancies.

5. Verify that the set of objectives is the leanest one possible, i.e., that everything necessary is present and everything superfluous has been removed.

Example:

General objective: Upon completion of this audiovisual training module and the practical assignments you will be able to produce, test, and revise a tutoring material.

Specific objectives: Specifically you will be able to demonstrate the following competencies:

1. SELECT a suitable skill to be taught through the tutoring materials.
2. OUTLINE a tutorial lesson on the selected skill.
3. PREPARE a set of flash cards for use in tutoring the selected skill.
4. DESIGN the strategy for a tutoring lesson.
5. DESIGN the strategy for individual items of the lesson.
6. PREPARE a performance aid for the tutor's reference.
7. TRY OUT the tutoring material with a child and make suitable revisions.
8. TRY OUT the tutoring material with a tutor and make suitable revisions.
9. TRY OUT the tutoring materials with a tutor and a child and make suitable revisions.

---

3. Construct a criterion item to match each objective.

WHY?

1. To form a base for verifying whether or not a specific objective has been attained.

2. To establish the central core for the response book.
3. To provide the milestones toward which the script for the audiotape is written.

WHEN?

1. Once the objectives have been specified.

WHO?

1. Generally speaking, this is the developer's responsibility. As with the objectives, it is wise to verify criterion items with the subject matter expert(s).

WHAT?

1. One separate card for each item.

HOW?

1. Construct an item which forces the trainee to perform precisely what the objectives state he/she will be able to do at the conclusion of the module.
2. Verify the item using the flowchart from Robert Mager's book, *Measuring Instructional Intent.* If you do not have this book, ask the following questions for each item?
   a. Does the item require the same performance stated in the objective?
   b. Is the main intent of the item the same as that of the objective?
   c. Is the trainee performance required in the item directly observable and measurable?
   d. Is the type of item (e.g., multiple choice, fill in the blanks, application), the best one for measuring attainment of the objective?

A "no" answer to any one of these questions signals the need for revision of the criterion item.

Example:
Objective: SELECT a suitable skill to be taught through the tutoring materials.
Criterion item:
What skill are you going to teach with your tutoring material? Describe it briefly here.

_____

_____

_____

_____

Objective: OUTLINE a tutorial lesson on the selected skill.
Criterion item:
Prepare an outline for your tutoring material by:
1. Writing down the specific objective.

2. Specifying the flashcard format at different levels of difficulty.

----

4. Write the script toward each criterion item.

WHY?

1. To provide the basis for the audio portion of the audio-visual training module.
2. To establish the links between and among the objectives.
3. To establish the scenarios, characters, dialogues, and narrative descriptions which will enhance the realism of the module and establish the context for the competencies to be acquired.

WHEN?

After the criterion items have been constructed and verified. The script generally requires a lengthy period of time to be written.

WHO?

The developer and/or the subject matter expert. If resources permit, a script writer. The person writing the script generally turns sections of it over to the subject-matter expert to obtain realistic examples, editorial feedback, and validity checks. The developer verifies that the script is instructionally relevant and within time and budget constraints. If there is an audio production person, he or she also checks the script for readability and the inclusion of sound effects.

WHAT?

Typewriter paper and a typewriter. Margins are set so that only the right half of each page contains the typed script, double or triple spaced. (The left half is for visual specifications.)

HOW?

1. Divide pages into two columns.
2. Type the text of the script on the right half of the page double or preferably triple-spaced, so that whoever reads it for recording will be able to follow the text easily.
3. Capitalize key words and phrases for emphasis. Place directions for pauses or sound effects in parentheses.
4. Keep the criterion items in front of you and write toward each item using a simple and straightforward style (no big or difficult-to-pronounce words).
5. Use a large number of clear-cut examples.
6. Ask questions frequently; give the trainee ample time to respond either mentally or overtly in the response book; provide feedback.
7. With interactive skills use dialogue; build checklists into the response book for trainees to assess what is going on during a dialogue.

8. Keep scripts brief. Get to the point quickly.

9. As the script develops, checklists, key points, performance aids, glossary terms, examples, and other important items will emerge. Keep these with the criterion items for inclusion into the response book later.

Example:

The first step in producing a tutoring material is to SELECT A SUITABLE SKILL you wish to teach to your children. The choice of this skill will depend upon your curriculum and the needs of the pupils in your classroom.

Not all skills can be effectively taught through tutoring materials. To ensure getting maximum benefit out of what you produce you will have to be certain that the skill will be USEFUL for more than one child.

For example, a tutoring material on how to write the name Tom Smith will be useful only for one child while another on recognizing road signs will be useful for many. (Pause 3 seconds)

The skill you want to teach should be of fundamental importance to the child's future learning. How to tell a particular story is not a very suitable topic. But recognizing different numerals is a prerequisite for many arithmetical operations. (Pause)

The skill you want to teach with the tutoring device should also be one which will require lots of drill practice. Addition facts, basic arithmetic operations, sight reading, and spelling are among some of the skills which fall into this category.

The skills must also be simple so that your tutors themselves do not have to learn them. Simple arithmetic operations and reading are examples of skills for which you have a large number of potential tutors.

It should be easy for the tutor to discriminate between correct and incorrect responses of the child. Obviously, such open-ended skills as expressing one's feelings or creative problem solving are not suitable for a brief tutoring aid.

Keeping these general suggestions in mind, select a suitable skill for the tutoring material you want to produce.

Turn to page 3 and write down your choice. Turn off the tape while you do this. Turn it back on after you have completed this task. (Signal tone.)

---

5. Design a visual storyboard which specifies the content of the slides.

WHY?

1. To provide the basis for the visual portion of the audio-visual training module.
2. To enhance the audio script by enlarging upon verbal explanations through visual images.
3. To establish the visual contexts, scenarios, and characters which add to the realism of the module and increase its meaningfulness for trainees.

WHEN?

Depending upon the designer either simultaneous with or just after the writing of the script. The majority of designers generally think verbally before they do so visually. However, as the script is written, visual design ideas which occur should be noted beside the text.

WHO?

The developer, script writer, photographer, and graphic artist. The developer may either lead off with a preliminary design or use brainstorming techniques to gather the most interesting and instructionally effective visual designs. As a general rule, those involved in the production should be encouraged to assist in the design.

WHAT?
1. Completed and edited scripts.
2. Visual storyboard cards. These can be in a variety of colors to represent the different types of shots.

HOW?
1. Design visuals which are relevant to the message you are trying to get across. The visual and audio text should form a *summative* combination—each reinforcing, strengthening, and clarifying the other.
2. To emphasize a particular point, specify a visual which carries the identical message as the audio. This *redundant* combination should be used sparingly and for key points only.
3. Avoid *interfering* combinations in which the visual is totally unrelated to the narration.
4. In specifying slide designs, draw a slash mark at the place in the script where the slide change occurs. Number each slash mark. In the left half of the script page write the same slide number and describe the visual.
5. Accompany the visual description with a simple sketch whenever possible.
6. Transfer visual designs to storyboard cards. It is best if each type of shot has a different colored card. Use the following simple classification for the different types of slides you may wish to use in your module.
    Live shot: A photograph of a scene or of live models engaged in an activity—usually requires props.

Propshot: A photograph of an object or objects especially arranged and lit to highlight specific features—usually a contrived arrangement of the objects.

Graphic: A photograph of a drawing, flowchart, or design—often includes words.

Caption: A photograph of a word or phrase.

Cartoon: A photograph of a freehand, stylized drawing.

Combination: Mixture of two or more of the above—often a liveshot or propshot with a superimposed caption.

Example:

82. "Select a suitable child." (CAPTION)

82/ You begin these tryouts by selecting a suitable child. Make sure that this child represents the type of children for whom the tutoring material is designed ...

83. Child doing a math page. Tutor sitting on floor holding flowchart and child. (LIVE SHOT)

83/ Take him through the materials by following your own flowchart and lesson strategy. As you tutor, watch for various problems ...

84. Child laboriously writing number in box on paper. (LIVE SHOT)

84/ For example, during our tryouts with the addition tutoring aid we originally required the child to write the sum of the two numbers in the box. But this slowed up the tutoring procedure so much that we decided to require only an oral response. There were a couple of other unanticipated problems during the tryouts ...

85. Child looking intently at handful of pennies. (LIVE SHOT)

85/ Originally, we used pennies for our counters, but we found that the children were so distracted by them that we had to shift to plain white poker chips ...

86. Two sets of cards: one with thin medium sized felt pen numbers, the

86/ Our original numbers were medium sized ones written with a felt pen. After the tryout we shifted to larger numbers written with a magic marker ...

other on larger
cards with bold
magic marker
numbers.
(PROPSHOT)

87. Flowchart:

87/ After four or five of these individual
tryouts with children and revisions, you
should be able to obtain consistent results
with your tutoring material. You are now
ready for a tryout with an actual tutor.

(GRAPHIC)

_____

6. Design the response book.

_____

WHY?

To provide the basis for the production of the trainee
response book complete with criterion items, performance
aids, checklists, flowcharts, glossary and references.

WHEN?

Once the script has been completed and all the content for
the response book has been specified.

WHO?

The developer.

WHAT?

1. Criterion items
2. Performance aids

3. Exercises
4. Feedback for the exercises
5. Glossary
6. List of references

HOW?

1. Place each criterion item on a separate page.
2. Prepare all additional items to be included in the response book separately and then integrate them among the criterion items.
3. Sequence the response book and number all pages.
4. Whenever completion of an exercise means that the trainee should return to the tape and slides, include a reminder on the page.
5. Repeat instructions for exercises from the audiotape in the response book as well.
6. Spread out the response book content so that plenty of space is available for trainee responses.
7. Design a durable cover, a table of contents page and a page containing the objectives of the module.

---

7. Produce the response book.

WHY?

1. To provide trainees with a series of criterion items and a place to practice skills and concepts presented in the audiovisual components of the module.
2. To leave the trainees with a permanent reference containing all sorts of aids relevant to the competencies of the module.

WHEN?

Once the design of the response book has been completed.

WHO?

The developer and printer.

WHAT?

1. Criterion items
2. Performance aids
3. Glossary
4. References
5. Follow-up activities
6. Objectives
7. Title page including disclaimers and credits
8. Cover

HOW?

1. Select the method of duplication which best fits your resources and requirements. Commonly available duplicating processes are described below.

Duplicating Processes

Process	Description
SPIRIT	Uses carbon masters. Permits a range of color choices; usually purple, blue, green, and black. The spirit duplicating machine is fairly inexpensive. It uses alcohol for reproducing. Minimal skill is required for this process so you can do it yourself.
STENCIL (mimeo)	Requires stencils especially designed for the brand of machine you have. Accepts typing (no ribbon) and drawings. Thermal machines and special electrical machines can produce stencils from typed and pasted up originals. You can draw on stencils with a stylus. The duplicating machine is moderately expensive. For best results the operator requires some training. Since ink is used, it can get messy. Changing colors is possible, but time-consuming.
PHOTO-COPYING	Usually called Xerox (though this is a brand name). This is essentially a "few copies" process. New machines can reproduce a large quantity of copies from an original

fairly rapidly. No training is required and there is no mess to clean up.

However, for more than a few copies, this is a very expensive process. Colors are out unless you have the very latest machine. Drawings and sketches come out beautifully. These machines do not reproduce certain kinds of blue.

OFFSET   If you have access to offset and need a large number of copies, use this process. Only an experienced operator can run the machine. You can get near perfect reproductions of the originals in a variety of colors (although that gets expensive). You usually have to wait several days for your copies. But for high volume, professional quality, if you have offset around, use it.

The following table compares the four duplicating processes in terms of cost, number of copies, the complexity of the process, the turnaround time, and the quality of the final product.

Comparison of Duplicating Processes

Process	Cost	No. of Copies	Complexity	Turnaround Time	Quality
Spirit	Very cheap about 20¢ per stencil and ½¢ per duplicated page.	Approx. 34 per stencil.	Simple to run.	30 copies per page requires about 5 min.	Some color, but not very professional looking.
Stencil (Mimeo)	Fairly cheap. About 45¢ per stencil and ¾¢ per page.	Approx. 200 good copies per stencil.	Moderately simple to do. Somewhat messy. If you've never tried it you'll need help.	200 copies per page requires about 10 min.	Print looks clean and drawings come out well, but color is a pretty big problem.

Photo-copying: Xerox, IBM, Olivetti, etc.	About 5¢ per page.	Any number.	Very simple.	100 copies requires about 10 min.	Gives an excellent reproduc-tion of the original, but no color.
Offset	High for small quantities but gets cheaper with volume.	Any number.	You need a profes-sional.	You have to get in line— usually a couple of days.	The best. You can re-produce pho-tos and all the color you want. But it's expensive!

2. Use a format that is efficient, inexpensive, and consumable for the take-home response book.
3. Update response books periodically as changes in the content occur.

----

8. Produce the audiotape.

WHY?
1. To provide trainees with the main instructional message.
2. To explain, describe, encourage, give feedback and advice, and direct the trainee's attention.
3. To lead the trainee from his entry level through to each criterion item in the response book.

WHEN?
Once the audioscript has been finalized, the recording studio and equipment prepared, and suitable readers found.

WHAT?
1. One script for each reader plus more for the audio engineer or sound man.
2. Recording equipment.

3. Recording studio or room.
4. Audiotape.
5. Music and sound effects.

WHO?
The audio engineer or sound man and readers.

HOW?
1. Select trained readers or at least persons with good recording voices.
2. Go minimally with two voices, preferably a female and a male to keep the trainees listening more attentively.
3. Use the best possible recording equipment available.
4. Use a good reel-to-reel tape recorder and at least two good microphones for your master tape.
5. For recording, select a room free from whirring motors, air conditioners, or outside noises.
6. For copying on to cassette, patch a cassette recorder to the reel-to-reel machine.
7. For multiple copies use a high speed duplicator which produces several copies in a very few minutes.
8. Keep in mind the following points when selecting audiotape:
   a. Recording tape is similar to photographic film: the older the tape, the lower its sensitivity.
   b. The larger the surface of the tape actually recorded on—full track compared to half track or half track compared to quarter track—the higher the quality of the recording.
   c. The thicker the recording tape is in terms of millimeters—the stronger it will be and the less likely a problem called "print through" will occur.
   d. A recording tape with a polyester base is stronger and more durable than an acetate based tape, although more expensive.

9. Keep in mind the following recording tips:
   a. The faster the recording speed (the more inches per second—IPS—of recording tape passing over the recording tape head) the higher the quality of the recording.
   b. When a tape copy is made from the original master tape, the copy is a "generation" removed from the master tape and the quality will be slightly lower.
   c. When using cassette tapes avoid any over 90 minutes long. Beside the tape being thinner, the additional length puts an extra strain on the cassette recorder.
   d. Most rooms tend to be "live" or reverberent and will produce a shallow echoing sound, so a carpeted, curtained, "dead" room will yield the best acoustics for recording.
   e. If your tape recorder has a "playback monitor" listen with your earphones to hear what the quality of the voices being recorded sound like coming through your tape recorder. This will help you adjust your balance and tone controls.

---

9. Produce the slides or filmstrip.

WHY?

1. To provide trainees with a set of visuals which accompanies and enlarges on the audio or even assumes the main instructional burden.
2. To build a new temporary visual environment for the trainee.
3. To act as a motivational device to maintain interest.
4. To focus the trainee's attention by "showing" while the audio does the "telling."

WHEN?

After the complete set of visual specifications has been

laid down, visual storyboard cards have been prepared and sorted, and a shooting schedule has been drawn up.

WHO?

The developer, photographer, and graphic artist.

WHAT?

1. Models
2. Settings
3. Props
4. Samples
5. Camera and equipment
6. Lights
7. Copystand
8. Photographic and graphic supplies
9. Model release forms.

HOW?

1. Assign each type of shot (e.g. live shot, graphic) to a visual storyboard card color. After specifying one visual per card, sort the cards into piles. Divide live shot cards by location.
2. Prepare a shooting schedule and shoot each pile of sorted cards separately.
3. Prepare to shoot from five to ten slides for each ultimately used.
4. Use the best camera available, preferably a 35mm single lens reflex camera with normal, close-up, and wide angle lenses.
5. Shoot titles and captions using plastic or cardboard letters laid on colored paper or words written on chalkboard. To obtain professional quality lettering, paste up photographically produced letters on white cardboard and copy on high contrast film.

6. For copy work, use tungsten lights, a copystand, and a 55mm macro lens. If these are not available, pin artwork on a bulletin board outdoors and shoot in sunlight.
7. Keep in mind the following suggestions when preparing your slides.
    a. Shoot close using lots of light to obtain crisp, clean, comprehensible visuals.
    b. Choose film to match the light source: indoor (tungsten) film for artificial lights and daylight film for sunlight. If your scene has both artificial and natural lighting, use film that matches the dominant light source.
    c. Some artificial light sources do not match well with indoor film. Daylight film works best where there is fluorescent lighting. With mercury vapor lighting, such as street lights, slides come out somewhat greenish. Special filters can eliminate this undesirable effect.
    d. Outdoor light changes with the time of day. Early morning and late afternoon gives slides a very reddish cast.
    e. Indoor film can be used outdoors if an 85B filter is placed over the lens. You have to open the lens an extra half stop if the camera does not have automatic metering.
    f. When lighting an indoor scene with floodlights, use a strong main light plus a smaller, weaker one to fill in shadow areas.
    g. For meter reading, use a Standard Grey Card to determine exposure. Be sure that the ASA setting on the meter and the camera matches the film ASA.
    h. If shutter speeds fall below 1/30 second, use a tripod to prevent camera shake.

i. F-stops such as 1.8, 2.8, 3.5, 4, and 5.6 do not have much *depth of focus*. Hence, subjects not in the *center of focus* may appear fuzzy. Subjects should be close together and centered when using these F-stops.

j. When shooting a scene, "bracket" your shots in one-half stop segments. This means shooting at the meter reading, one-half stop higher, and one-half stop lower.

k. Have your film processed by a reputable company, such as Kodak. Your local drugstore's labs may ruin irreplaceable shots.

l. Kodak, by special processing, can increase the ASA of your film. This is useful for very low light conditions, but you have to request this treatment specifically.

10. Assemble the total module.

WHY?

1. To ensure that all three components form a single harmonious instructional package.
2. To verify that the visuals are consistent with the audiotape.
3. To synchronize audio and visual.

WHEN?

Once all components have been produced, edited, the final visual selections made, and the response books bound.

WHO?

The developer and a "naive" outsider.

WHAT?

1. The final selected slides.
2. The bound response book.
3. The edited audiotape.
4. Synchronizing equipment.

HOW?

1. If you have a synchronized system (i.e., your machine can advance slides or filmstrip automatically), pulse your tape. Refer to the operating manual of your specific piece of equipment for detailed instructions.

2. Keep in mind the following suggestions for working with automatic synchronization:

    a. The tone you use to advance the visuals should be of short duration (about 1/4 second) to avoid tripping the advance mechanism more than once.

    b. It is advisable to add the automatic-advance tones after the recording of narration, the addition of sound effects and music, and the organization of slides have been completed.

    c. Always check the audiovisual synchronization to be sure that the visuals are correctly advancing and that no tones have been accidentally omitted or extra ones included.

3. If you do not have automatic synchronization capabilities, use a tone to signal the trainee to shift to the next slide. There are a large variety of ways you can do this; here are four common techniques:

    a. Cricket: This is a simple clicker device that gives a clean, clear, and distinct signal for advancing visuals. It is obtainable for a few cents especially around Halloween time. The narrators can "click" the cricket each time there is a slide change. (Cost: Approximately 25¢ - 50¢.)

    b. Door-chime: This can be purchased for a few dollars at any hardware store. By connecting it to an electric outlet (or battery) a pleasant signal is obtained. The narrators can depress the button while reading. (Cost: approximately $5 - $10.)

    c. 1000_{Hz} tone: This tone comes from a "bench signal

generator" (also called a "variable audio oscillator") that provides a broad range of signals. It is easy to operate and can usually be obtained from an electronics department. (Cost: $150 - $350.)

d. Xylophone: If you have access to one of these, you can select the tone which sounds most pleasant to you. Toy xylophones also produce clear, usable signals. (Cost: Approximately $5 - $25.)

4. To assemble the components of your module, place your slides in their final sequence into a tray. Turn on the tape. Each time the tape tells the trainee to refer to the response book, stop the tape and check the page number. Make sure slides and tape are in "synch."

5. Because the developer's familiarity with the material can make him/her overlook inconsistencies or confusing instructions, have a "naive" person work through the module.

Checklist for Developing Audiovisual Training Modules

1. Task analysis of selected topic completed
   —prerequisite tasks specified
   —superfluous items eliminated
   —overlooked items added
2. Subtasks converted to performance objectives
   —overall objectives specified
   —specific objectives stated
   —objectives arranged in an instructional sequence
3. Criterion items constructed
   —items require the same performance as the objective
   —trainee performance is directly observable and measurable
   —types of items are the best ones for measuring attainment of objectives

4. Script written
   —each section leads directly to criterion item
   —sufficient clear-cut examples included
   —questions asked frequently
   —feedback included
   —music, sound effects, and audio directions specified
5. Visual storyboard designed
   —visuals specified beside relevant audioscript text
   —visuals specifications transcribed to cards
   —no interfering combinations included
6. Response book designed
   —criterion items placed on separate pages
   —performance aids designed
   —glossary prepared
   —references selected
   —cover, title page, contents, objectives prepared
   —pages sequenced and numbered
7. Response book produced
   —duplicating process selected
   —format selected
   —multiple copies produced
   —response books bound
8. Audiotape produced
   —readers selected
   —equipment prepared
   —recording studio/room prepared
   —voices recorded
   —music and sound effects added
   —audiotape edited
9. Slides produced
   —shooting schedule prepared
   —camera equipment and supplies prepared
   —graphics and captions designed
   —slides shot

      –final slides selected

10. Total module assembled
      –audiotape and visuals checked against each other and against response book
      –audio and visuals synchronized
      –assembly checked by "naive" outsider

VI.

RESOURCES

Audiovisual training modules are not new—only the term and perhaps the approach taken in this book are new. Excellent examples of audiovisual training modules can be purchased from the Center for Innovation in Teaching the Handicapped, Indiana University, Bloomington, Indiana 47401. Some additional resources you may want to look into are as follows:

BOOKS

Crowhurst, N. H. *A B C's of Tape Recording*. Indianapolis, Indiana: Howard W. Sams & Company and the Bobbs-Merrill Company, 1971.

Rhode, R. B. and F. H. McCall. *Introduction to Photography*. New York, New York: The Macmillan Company, 1971.

BOOKLETS

Kodak Publications: *Adventures in Existing-Light Photography*. AC-44.

Basic Tilting and Animation for Motion Pictures, S-21.

Color as Seen and Photographed, E-74.

Copying, M-21.

Kodak Color Films for Still Cameras, AE-41.

Producing Slides and Filmstrips, S-8.
Slides with a Purpose for Business and Education.
Suggestions for Loading and Handling 35mm Cameras, AE-46.
Rochester, New York: Eastman Kodak Company.

Lord, J. and R. H. Larson. *Handbook for the Production of 35mm Sound Filmstrips (3rd edition).* St. Charles, Illinois: DuKane Corporation, Audiovisual Division, 1971.

Pett, D. W. *Copying and Duplicating Processes.* Bloomington, Indiana: Audiovisual Center, Indiana University, 1974.

ARTICLES

Stolovitch, H. D. How to Produce Audiovisual Training Modules, *NSPI Journal*, May 1976.

Stolovitch, H. D. Getting into Production. *NSPI Journal*, June 1976.

Stolovitch, H. D. Evaluating Your Product. *NSPI Journal*, July 1976.

AUDIOVISUAL TRAINING MODULE

Stolovitch, H. D. *How to Develop Audiovisual Training Modules.* Bloomington, Indiana: Center for Innovation in Teaching the Handicapped, 1976.

WORKSHOP

The author conducts workshops varying from two to five days on developing audiovisual training modules.

HAROLD D. STOLOVITCH has had a career in education that spans the elementary, secondary, and university levels and that spreads across several countries, including Cameroun in West Africa, the United States, and Canada. He is currently on the faculty of the Universite de Montreal, where he teaches and directs the master's programs in educational technology. He is also engaged in research on the learner verification and revision process, especially as it concerns non-print materials used in the public schools. He has been responsible for a large scale instructional development project at the Center for Innovation in Teaching the Handicapped, Indiana University, and has participated in the production of a number of audiovisual training modules, simulations and games, and other mediated materials. His work takes him into the industrial and military world, where he consults and runs workshops on a variety of instructional development topics. His publications include books on instructional simulation games, games with the pocket calculator, and audiovisual training modules. He has also published a number of articles and mediated materials on various aspects of instructional development.